1 PIANO, 4 HANDS

VOLUME 20

WICKED

MUSIC AND LYRICS BY STEPHEN SCHWARTZ

Arranged by Carol Klose

T0039512

Speed • Pitch • Balance • Loop

To access audio, visit:
www.halleonard.com/mylibrary

3739-1895-5696-6313

ISBN 978-1-4234-3644-7

Visit Hal Leonard Online at
www.halleonard.com

Contact us:
Hal Leonard
7777 West Bluemound Road
Milwaukee, WI 53213
Email: info@halleonard.com

In Europe, contact:
Hal Leonard Europe Limited
42 Wigmore Street
Marylebone, London, W1U 2RN
Email: info@halleonardeurope.com

In Australia, contact:
Hal Leonard Australia Pty. Ltd.
4 Lentara Court
Cheltenham, Victoria, 3192 Australia
Email: info@halleonard.com.au

THE WIZARD AND I

SECONDO

Music and Lyrics by
STEPHEN SCHWARTZ

THE WIZARD AND I

PRIMO

Music and Lyrics by
STEPHEN SCHWARTZ

Pulsing with excitement

With light pedal

SECONDO

SECONDO

SECONDO

WHAT IS THIS FEELING?

SECONDO

Music and Lyrics by
STEPHEN SCHWARTZ

Allegro, jauntily pugnacious

WHAT IS THIS FEELING?

PRIMO

Music and Lyrics by
STEPHEN SCHWARTZ

Allegro, jauntily pugnacious

SECONDO

SECONDO

DANCING THROUGH LIFE

SECONDO

Music and Lyrics by
STEPHEN SCHWARTZ

Freely

p ad lib.

pp

With light pedal

p

p

poco rit.

8vb -|

DANCING THROUGH LIFE

PRIMO

Music and Lyrics by
STEPHEN SCHWARTZ

SECONDO

SECONDO

POPULAR

SECONDO

Music and Lyrics by
STEPHEN SCHWARTZ

Sweetly

With pedal

POPULAR

PRIMO

Music and Lyrics by
STEPHEN SCHWARTZ

SECONDO

PRIMO

I'M NOT THAT GIRL

SECONDO

Music and Lyrics by
STEPHEN SCHWARTZ

Sweetly and steadily, like a music box

With pedal

I'M NOT THAT GIRL

PRIMO

Music and Lyrics by
STEPHEN SCHWARTZ

Sweetly and steadily, like a music box

PRIMO

Tempo I

DEFYING GRAVITY

SECONDO

Music and Lyrics by
STEPHEN SCHWARTZ

Freely, with quiet intensity

With pedal

DEFYING GRAVITY

PRIMO

Music and Lyrics by
STEPHEN SCHWARTZ

Freely, with quiet intensity

SECONDO

Moderato, dreamily

SECONDO

rall.   a tempo

mp

mf

107

With determination

rall.

111

8va

pp *sub.*

115

(8va)

rall.

ff *a tempo*

119

(8va)

8va

rall.

I COULDN'T BE HAPPIER

SECONDO

Music and Lyrics by
STEPHEN SCHWARTZ

Andante, melancholy

With pedal

I COULDN'T BE HAPPIER

PRIMO

Music and Lyrics by
STEPHEN SCHWARTZ

SECONDO

PRIMO

SECONDO

FOR GOOD

SECONDO

Music and Lyrics by
STEPHEN SCHWARTZ

Tenderly, poco rubato

FOR GOOD

PRIMO

Music and Lyrics by
STEPHEN SCHWARTZ

SECONDO

PIANO FOR TWO
A Variety of Piano Duets from Hal Leonard

ADELE FOR PIANO DUET
Intermediate Level

Eight of Adele's biggest hits arranged especially for intermediate piano duet! Featuring: Chasing Pavements • Hello • Make You Feel My Love • Rolling in the Deep • Set Fire to the Rain • Skyfall • Someone Like You • When We Were Young.
00172162 1 Piano, 4 Hands $14.99

THE BEATLES FOR PIANO DUET
Intermediate Level
arr. Eric Baumgartner

Eight great Beatles' songs arranged for piano duet! Titles: Blackbird • Come Together • In My Life • Lucy in the Sky with Diamonds • Michelle • Ob-la-di, Ob-la-da • While My Guitar Gently Weeps • Yellow Submarine.
00275877 1 Piano, 4 Hands $14.99

THE BIG BOOK OF PIANO DUETS

24 great piano duet arrangements! Includes: Beauty and the Beast • Clocks • Edelweiss • Georgia on My Mind • He's a Pirate • Let It Go • Linus and Lucy • Moon River • Yellow Submarine • You are the Sunshine of My Life • and more!
00232851 1 Piano, 4 Hands $14.99

CONTEMPORARY DISNEY DUETS
Intermediate Level

8 great Disney duets: Evermore (from Beauty and the Beast) • How Does a Moment Last Forever (from Beauty and the Beast) • How Far I'll Go (from Moana) • Lava • Let It Go (from Frozen) • Proud Corazon (from Coco) • Remember Me (from Coco) • You're Welcome (from Moana).
00285562 1 Piano, 4 Hands $12.99

EASY CLASSICAL DUETS
Book/Online Audio
Willis Music

7 great piano duets to perform at a recital, play-for-fun, or sightread: By the Beautiful Blue Danube (Strauss) • Eine kleine Nachtmusik (Mozart) • Hungarian Rhapsody No. 5 (Liszt) • Morning from Peer Gynt (Grieg) • Rondeau (Mouret) • Sleeping Beauty Waltz (Tchaikovsky) • Surprise Symphony (Haydn). Includes online audio tracks for the primo and secondo part for download or streaming.
00145767 1 Piano, 4 Hands $10.99

FAVORITE DISNEY SONGS FOR PIANO DUET
Early Intermediate Level

8 great Disney songs creatively arranged for piano duet: Can You Feel the Love Tonight • Do You Want to Build a Snowman • A Dream Is a Wish Your Heart Makes • Supercalifragilisticexpialidocious • That's How You Know • When Will My Life Begin? • You'll Be in My Heart • You've Got a Friend in Me.
00285563 1 Piano, 4 Hands $12.99

FIRST 50 PIANO DUETS YOU SHOULD PLAY

Includes: Autumn Leaves • Bridge over Troubled Water • Chopsticks • Fields of Gold • Hallelujah • Imagine • Lean on Me • Theme from "New York, New York" • Over the Rainbow • Peaceful Easy Feeling • Singin' in the Rain • A Thousand Years • What the World Needs Now Is Love • You Raise Me Up • and more.
00276571 1 Piano, 4 Hands $19.99

GOSPEL DUETS
The Phillip Keveren Series

Eight inspiring hymns arranged by Phillip Keveren for one piano, four hands, including: Church in the Wildwood • His Eye Is on the Sparrow • In the Garden • Just a Closer Walk with Thee • The Old Rugged Cross • Shall We Gather at the River? • There Is Power in the Blood • When the Roll Is Called up Yonder.
00295099 1 Piano, 4 Hands $12.99

THE GREATEST SHOWMAN
by Benj Pasek & Justin Paul
Intermediate Level

Creative piano duet arrangements for the songs: Come Alive • From Now On • The Greatest Show • A Million Dreams • Never Enough • The Other Side • Rewrite the Stars • This Is Me • Tightrope.
00295078 1 Piano, 4 Hands $16.99

BILLY JOEL FOR PIANO DUET
Intermediate Level

8 of the Piano Man's greatest hits – perfect as recital encores, or just for fun! Titles: It's Still Rock and Roll to Me • Just the Way You Are • The Longest Time • My Life • New York State of Mind • Piano Man • She's Always a Woman • Uptown Girl.
00141139 1 Piano, 4 Hands $14.99

HEART AND SOUL & OTHER DUET FAVORITES

8 fun duets arranged for two people playing on one piano. Includes: Any Dream Will Do • Chopsticks • Heart and Soul • Music! Music! Music! (Put Another Nickel In) • On Top of Spaghetti • Raiders March • The Rainbow Connection • Y.M.C.A..
00290541 1 Piano, 4 Hands $10.99

RHAPSODY IN BLUE
George Gershwin/
arr. Brent Edstrom

Originally written for piano and jazz band, "Rhapsody in Blue" was later orchestrated by Ferde Grofe. This intimate adaptation for piano duet delivers access to advancing pianists and provides an exciting musical collaboration and adventure!
00125150 1 Piano, 4 Hands $12.99

RIVER FLOWS IN YOU & OTHER SONGS FOR PIANO DUET
Intermediate Level

10 great songs including the title song and: All of Me (Piano Guys) • Bella's Lullaby • Beyond • Chariots of Fire • Dawn • Forrest Gump - Main Title (Feather Theme) • Primavera • Somewhere in Time • Watermark.
00141055 1 Piano, 4 Hands $12.99

TOP HITS FOR EASY PIANO DUET
Book/Online Audio
arr. David Pearl

10 great songs with backing tracks: Despacito (Justin Bieber ft. Luis Fonsi & Daddy Yankee) • Havana (Camila Cabello ft. Young Thug • High Hopes (Panic! At the Disco) • A Million Dreams (The Greatest Showman) • Perfect (Ed Sheeran) • Senorita (Camila Cabello & Shawn Mendes) • Shallow (Lady Gaga & Bradley Cooper) • Someone You Loved (Lewis Capaldi) • Speechless (Aladdin) • Sucker (Jonas Brothers).
00326133 1 Piano, 4 Hands $12.99

HAL•LEONARD®
www.halleonard.com